HOW TO PLAY THE BAGPIPES

A Step-by-Step Guide to Learning the Basics, Reading Music and Playing Songs with Audio Recordings

By: Jason Randall

Table of Contents

Chapter 1: Overview..1

What is a Bagpipe? How did it get its name? 1

The Origin of Bagpipes 3

How long does it take to learn the bagpipes?.......................4

The purpose of using a practice chanter 6

Chapter 2: How to Select and Purchase the Correct Practice Chanter and Bagpipes for Beginners?................................8

Practice Chanter..8

Length: Regular and Long (similar to pipe chanter) 8

Recommendations 9

Bagpipes..10

Selecting your bagpipes 10

Synthetic vs. Skin Bags 10

Reeds..11

Blackwood or polypenco pipe chanter 13

Recommendations on popular bagpipe brands..................14

Engraving patterns: Thistle and Celtic 14

The importance of quality bagpipes 15

Chapter 3: Learn the Music Theory and Notes – Developing Musical Vocabulary 17

Understand the basic building blocks of music 17

How to read a music sheet? 17

Time signatures 19

Details about different musical notes 19

Learn about musical alphabets and basic notes 22

Learn about musicianship skills 22

Chapter 4: Playing Notes/Songs on the Practice Chanter 25

You can play only nine notes on a bagpipe. 25

One octave + 1 note -> nine notes (G, A, B, C, D, E, F, G, A) –
low G to high G and high A 25

No flats or sharps in Bagpipe music 26

Practice playing notes (G, A, B, C, D, E, F, G, A) on the Chanter: 26

Practice finger positioning for each note 26

Exercises (with pictorial representations and music sheet) 29

Practice playing simple songs by memorizing the notes 32

Exercises (with pictorial representations and music sheet) 32

Use practice chanters to learn the notes 33

The purpose of electronic chanters. 33

**Chapter 5: Bagpipe Basics - Parts of a Bagpipe (with pictorial
representations)** 35

Bag 35

Blowstick/blowpipe 36

Drones 37

One Bass Drone - Plays low A 38

Two Tenor Drones - Plays middle A 39

Drone Cords 39

Chanter..40

Four Reeds – A device that produces a tone due to vibration
(caused by airflow)...40

Chapter 6: Learning the Bagpipe Basics...............43

How to set up your bagpipes.................................43

Learning how to start the bagpipes and hold them correctly..........45

Learning to control your breath while blowing into the blowpipe ..47

Understand that air, pressure, and deflation are directly related to
the type of bag (skin or synthetic) 48

Practice controlling your breath and left arm.....................48

Learn how to properly close the eight holes in the chanter with your
left and right fingers 48

Briefly understand the mechanics of how a bagpipe makes a sound. 49

Briefly understand how to tune your drones.....................49

Chapter 7: Introduction to Intermediate Techniques 51

Learn the striking technique (seems advanced but something useful
while playing in a band) 51

Learning how to play "D throw".................................52

Quick introduction to other embellishments 53

Chapter 8: Caring For Your Bagpipes.....................55

The Bag..55

Water trap & moisture control..................................55

Airtight – hemp wax thread 56

General maintenance 56

Chapter 9: Preparing to Play in a Pipeband 57

Different types of songs in Bagpipe music...........................57

Music sheet for Popular melodies and songs (all-time favorites).....59

Exercises to Build Techniques and to play in a band........................62

Chapter 10: Conclusion..65

Appendix..67

Additional Resources 67

Throughout this book there are musical examples and audio recordings to follow along with on your journey to learn how to play the Bagpipes.

Whenever you see the following outline:

```
Listening Example #1: Example of Different Musical Notes
```

Please follow along with the recordings at the Sound Cloud link below or search on Sound Cloud for "How to Play the Bagpipes".

https://soundcloud.com/jason_randall/sets/how-to-play-the-bagpipes

Chapter 1

Overview

Taking the first step to learning the bagpipes is the biggest one, so congratulations on deciding to start! The bagpipes have a long-standing history and are one of those instruments that, although not played by everyone, offer a truly unique experience for those who decide to play.

The bagpipes are Scottish instruments commonly played at various events such as weddings, funerals, and war memorial days. There are also bagpipe competitions and the Scottish much beloved, Ceilidh, where the bagpipes are, of course, going to come out. Learning to play the bagpipes is often much more than just learning how to play. It's about understanding the history, the culture, and the traditions surrounding this beautiful instrument.

This book will teach you everything you need to know, from learning how to set your bagpipes to playing simple tunes on the practice chanter and then playing tunes on the bagpipes themselves.

What is a Bagpipe? How did it get its name?

The bagpipes are a woodwind musical instrument that produces sounds through four enclosed reeds through which air is constantly pushed out from the bag. The sounds from the bagpipes come from two main areas; the "chanter" and the "drones." The chanter is where the player plays the tune with their fingers, and the drones are the tall pipes at the top that produce the background sound.

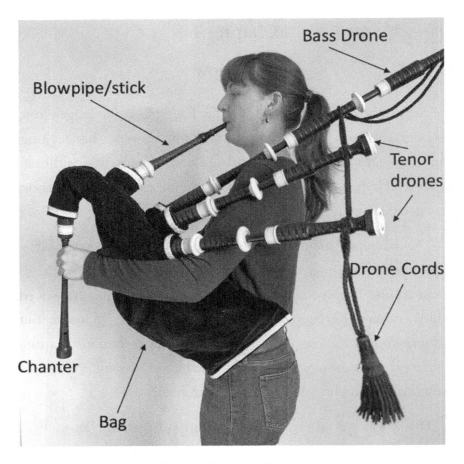

Player holding a set of bagpipes

The history of the name can be linked back to the Gaelic word for bagpipe, "P'iob mho'r," which means "big pipe." Although the term "bagpipe" is used, an equally correct and more common term is "bagpipes," which pipers use to describe their instrument. Bagpipes are called bagpipes due to their structure as musical instruments. The instrument is made of pipes and a bag, hence, bagpipes.

The Origin of Bagpipes

The bagpipes are commonly known as Scottish instruments. In fact, the bagpipes are Scotland's national instrument today; however, many still debate its actual origin. Some historians believe that the bagpipes, originating in ancient Egypt, were brought into Scotland by Roman Legions. Other historians have speculated that bagpipes were brought to Scotland from Ireland. According to Historic UK, the "pipers of Thebes" were reportedly playing the bagpipes from as early as 400 BC. Theirs had a bag made from dog skin and a chanter made of bone.

These original bagpipes are thought to have existed in many countries worldwide. Although several adaptations and changes may have occurred, the primary structural components of the bagpipes remained the same with a bag, drones (one or more), and a chanter. Variations in materials used to construct each component also varied between countries.

The development of the bagpipes into their current form today, however, was done by the "Highlanders." They established the bagpipes as Scotland's national instrument. It is thought that these bagpipes developed by the Highlanders only consisted of one drone, with the second being added in the late 1500s and a third in the early 1700s.

Today, bagpipes are played around the world, and several countries with strong ties to Scotland have kept bagpipes as part of their tradition. Canada, New Zealand, and Australia are all former British colonies with a strong Scottish bagpipe presence in their country, including in their militaries.

How long does it take to learn the bagpipes?

When you start your bagpipe learning adventure, there are various stages that you will go through to learn this instrument. Unlike some other instruments, bagpipes are characterized as more challenging instruments to learn due to the multi-tasking involved while playing the instrument. Bagpipes require the player to blow and squeeze the bag to maintain a constant pressure, as well as play the tunes on the chanter. Not only do you have to be able to play the tunes on the chanter, but you also need to be what we call "piping fit" to be able to blow through a series of tunes on the bagpipes. Like athletes, bagpipers must keep in shape for competitions and other events.

Depending on whom you talk to about learning how to play the bagpipes, it can take an average of six months to learn enough to get to a position where you can play tunes on the bagpipes. More complicated tunes will require years of training to master.

Players will start by mastering simple tunes on a practice chanter before moving on to something commonly referred to as a "goose," which is a bagpipe bag with the chanter, and then onto a full set of bagpipes. Once players get on to a full set of bagpipes, there are various ways to make playing simpler, such as blocking off one or multiple drones. This can help beginners build up to the full set.

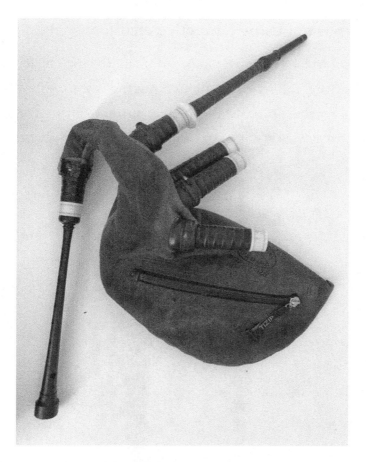

Typical set-up for a "goose." The three drones can be blocked off using rubber corks. Using this set-up can be an easy way for new players to get used to blowing into and squeezing the bag and playing the chanter at the same time.

Bagpipes can be a very challenging instrument to learn; however, if you follow the guidelines and take small steps building up to playing the bagpipes, you will be there in no time!

The purpose of using a practice chanter

Starting to learn the bagpipes can be incredibly challenging. If you start with a full set of bagpipes from the get-go, you will likely struggle to make progress and may even quit out of frustration. The easier way to learn is by starting with a practice chanter.

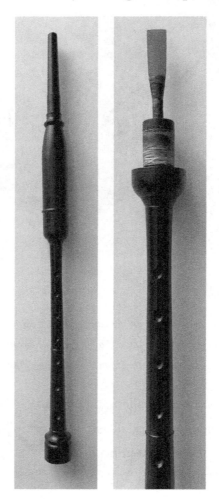

Practice Chanter and plastic reed (example of a regular practice chanter)

A practice chanter is a small sub-version of a full set of bagpipes in that it does not contain the pipes or bag. It is simply the part of the bagpipes you use to play the tunes with your fingers. Beginner players use a practice chanter to learn how to play simple tunes while blowing into the mouthpiece to create noise, similar to a recorder. Inside the chanter is a small reed that creates the sound.

Practice chanters are an excellent way for beginner players to get down the basics of how to play simple tunes before moving on to the next stage. Just playing the chanter itself may take some time for new players to master, but don't worry; throughout this e-book, we will take you through the basics of beginning your bagpipe playing journey and help you make a success out of it.

Chapter 2

How to Select and Purchase the Correct Practice Chanter and Bagpipes for Beginners?

Practice Chanter

When you start learning how to play the bagpipes, the first thing that you are going to want to buy is a practice chanter. If you aren't fully committed to buying a full set of bagpipes just yet, you can settle for just buying a practice chanter to get you started.

Length: Regular and Long (similar to pipe chanter)

There are two different types of practice chanters and slight variations between different brands that you may find. The longer practice chanter is generally closer to a bagpipe chanter and the finger spacing is slightly wider. Even with the longer chanter, there will still be some adjustments when you move onto the bagpipe chanter. As such, at the end of the day, if you are a beginner there is no real advantages to using a longer practice chanter.

A regular chanter can be easier to learn as the finger spacing is slightly narrower but with time, you will get used to switching between a practice chanter and a bagpipe chanter. Even though the longer practice chanter mimics the actual bagpipe chanter that you will end up playing later on, I would still recommend opting for a regular size. Learning some of the embellishments may be a little bit more difficult to learn for a beginner and the slightly narrower spacing on the regular size would suit most beginners to learn.

If it is a child that is beginning, there are also junior sizes available.

Recommendations

I would recommend just getting whatever chanter you can get your hands on and is in your price range. As a beginner, there are no real advantages to having a more expensive/fancy practice chanter. When you end up playing with others in bands, competitions, and events, it will be the bagpipes that you will be playing on, not the practice chanter.

Practice chanters are typically made with either plastic or wooden material and all chanters will have a plastic reed (wooden reed is only for a bagpipe chanter). Plastic chanters are cheaper and most beginners will start with a plastic chanter and then buy a nicer wooden practice chanter later on in their career.

Most bagpiping stores will sell practice chanters. I would recommend buying a standard regular plastic practice chanter to get going. R. C. Hardie & Co and McCallum Bagpipes both have some nice options for practice chanters but it really doesn't matter too much.

Bagpipes

Selecting your bagpipes

Now, if you are looking to buy a set of bagpipes, there are many things that you should consider looking for. Bagpipes, even the cheapest options, are not all that cheap and there are a variety of factors that you should consider when you are looking at the options.

When you start looking for bagpipes to buy, you should be careful and know exactly what you are buying. It is pretty common that if you are going to buy "bagpipes" from a dealer, what you are actually buying is the drones and mouth piece. The bag, drone reeds, chanter, and chanter reeds are sold separately as bagpipers have different tastes when it comes to what they want.

The simplest option would be to buy a complete kit from your local bagpipe shop that comes with everything that you need to get started. However, you may also want to consider what you are actually buying.

Something else that you could do is rent a set of bagpipes to see if you like how they feel to play. Also, if there is a local pipeband that you are looking to join, many of the pipers will likely have different bagpipes that you could try to see what you like.

Synthetic vs. Skin Bags

The other decision that you will have to make is whether you want to go for a synthetic or skin (also known as hide) bag. There are pros and cons to both of these types of bags and how they feel when you play them is very different.

A synthetic bag is usually made from a breathable-materials that is designed for bagpipe bags. They usually require little to no maintenance and are easily stored. You can take your pipes out after being stored for long periods of time and they will still play the same.

Skin bags on the other hand need more maintenance and attention to keep them in the best condition. Skin bags need to be regularly seasoned to make sure they don't dry out and ruin the leather. This is important for not only the quality of sound but maintaining a good seal. You certainly don't want any leaks within your system. The environment and climate are also going to have an effect on how often you need to season your bag.

The other option you could consider which is becoming increasing common is a hybrid bag. Generally, this is a faux leather bag that is technically synthetic but really is more similar to a skin bag. These can be great options if you are looking for that hide bag feel but don't want an actual skin bag.

Choosing a synthetic vs. skin bag is entirely up to you and what you think you are going to be using the bagpipes for. The skin bags typically help to provide a more harmonic and broader sound with more vibrancy, so they are typically more common amongst bagpipers.

Reeds

You are going to need to buy 4 reeds for your set-up; 3 drone reeds and 1 pipe chanter reed. If you have chosen a fully-set up bagpipe, you won't need to worry about selecting drone reeds but you may need to consider them in the future. As a beginner, <u>Ezeedrone</u> bagpipe reeds can be a great place to start. Like the name suggests, they are easy to use and create a great overall sound for your drones. If you are looking for something a bit better, the original <u>Canning drone reeds</u> (with carbon fibre bass) is a great way to go.

As for pipe chanter reeds, there isn't too much variation here. Just make sure that you are getting a wooden pipe chanter reed. The plastic ones are for your practice chanter only. The main thing to note about the wooden chanter reeds is that the overall thickness of the reed will determine how difficult it is to play. A thicker reed will be more difficult to play and a thinner one will be easier to play. You will probably need to adjust the thickness of these reeds when you are first starting out, so it might pay to purchase a few. Just remember, you can always shave more wood off but you can't add it back on.

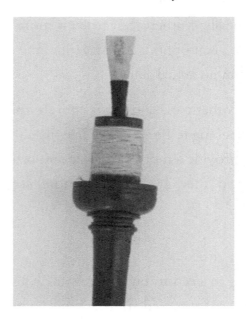

Wooden reed on pipe chanter

Blackwood or polypenco pipe chanter

Like we talked about with the practice chanter, you can either purchase a wooden (blackwood) or plastic bagpipe chanter too. As you can imagine, a blackwood pipe chanter is probably going to create a better-quality sound than a polypenco chanter. However, the polypenco chanters tend to be louder than the blackwoods, less expensive, and easier to take care of. As a beginner, I would recommend starting out with a polypenco pipe chanter.

Many of the popular bagpipe brands also sell polypenco pipe chanters and bagpipes already set up will come with one.

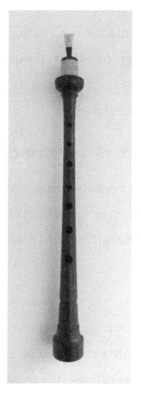

Blackwood bagpipe chanter with wood reed

Recommendations on popular bagpipe brands

There are plenty of bagpipe brands out there on the market but most of the best brands are the ones that are made in Scotland or have strong Scottish influence.

Some of the most popular bagpipe brands include McCallum Bagpipes, MacLellan Bagpipes, R. G. Hardie & Co, Duncan MacRae Bagpipes, Wallace Bagpipes (sponsor the Red Hot Chilli Pipers), and David Naill & Co.

All of these brands make and produce bagpipes to the highest quality. When you are choosing a new set of bagpipes, the drones and mouth piece are generally made of wood (e.g., blackwood) with either ivory (or imitation ivory) or silver mounts and connections. It depends on how much you are wanting to spend and what style of bagpipes that you are looking for.

Engraving patterns: Thistle and Celtic

If you choose a set of bagpipes that have silver (nickel or brass) connections and mounts, you will also have the option to engrave these. The two most common styles of engraving are Thistle and Celtic styles.

The biggest decision that you will have to make is first is choosing if you want to have silver on your bagpipes or not. Engraving is something that can only be done on silver (or other metal alloys) connections and tips. It cannot be done if you choose completely wood or ivory bagpipes.

Engraving is also something that can be done at a later date if you are not sure if you want it or which style to choose. You can purchase your bagpipes and then send them off later for engraving once you have decided if and what style you might want.

The two styles (Thistle and Celtic), look very different but are both rooted in Scottish heritage. One or the other isn't necessarily better, it all up to personal preference and the way that you want your bagpipes to look.

Not only can the engraving be a great way to make your bagpipes look more professional, it can also make them look cleaner. If you purchase a set of bagpipes without engraving but with silver, you will find that it is pretty easy for the silver to get dirty, smudges, or even tarnish a little bit. With the engraving, some of these can be masked a little bit. It is really easy to get the dirt, smudges, and mild tarnish out of the silver using a jewelry cloth.

The importance of quality bagpipes

The quality of your bagpipes is important for the quality of sound that you are looking for. Of course, the higher the price is generally correlated with a better sounding instrument. The bagpipes are one of those instruments that generally ages well and the sound quality gets better the older they become. Playing the bagpipes regularly will also increase the sound quality. So, if you opt for a new set of bagpipes, the more you play them, the better they are going to sound.

Purchasing a set of well-crafted bagpipes will also be something that will be able to stay in your family for generation. It is really easily to replace the parts of the bagpipes that wear quicker, such as the bag, but a really nice set of pipes (drones + blowpipe) will last a very long time.

Chapter 3

Learn the Music Theory and Notes – Developing Musical Vocabulary

Before we begin looking at how to play the practice chanter, it is worth understanding the basics of music theory and begin learning how to read sheet music. These basic skills will help you in the next section when we start to learn to play practice exercises from sheet music.

Understand the basic building blocks of music

When we break down the basic building blocks of music, this usually comes down to musical notes, rhythm, key signatures, melody, harmony, and chords. Of course, there are a lot of other things to it.

How to read a music sheet?

To understand how to read sheet music, there is a few things you first need to understand. Firstly, in bagpipe music (and almost every other instrument), musical notes are read on what is called "staff." The word "staff" is used to describe the 5 horizontal lines and 4 spaces where musical notes are placed. Staff is what it is commonly known as in the US, you may also see it referred to as stave which is the British English. Staves is the plural version in both cases.

On this figure you may also notice a few other features. The vertical lines are known as bar lines which are used to divide the staff into "bars." The other thing you will notice is the Treble Clef. The treble clef is the symbol that is used to tell the player which notes we are going to play. There are three types of clefs, but you will only see a treble clef in bagpipe music. The final thing that you will notice on sheet music is a time signature. We will go into more detail on time signatures in the next section.

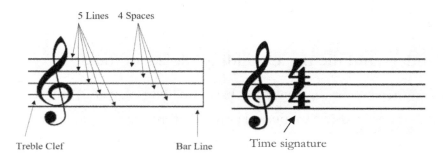

Choosing the bagpipes actually makes understanding some of the basic building blocks of music simpler. As noted earlier, there is only one scale (D major) that contains only 12 notes to learn on the bagpipes. In other sheet music, you will likely see either sharps (#) or flats (b) located between the clef and time signature. The number of sharps or flats will denote the "key" of which the music shall be played in. As D major is the only key you will ever play in on the bagpipes, you will almost ever see a key signature on any sheet music. It should always be inferred that we will be playing the key of D major. This makes life a lot similar as you will never have to think about different scales like you would with other instruments.

Time signatures

The time signature tells you how many notes are in each bar and the bottom number tells us what note gets the beat. In the case for the time signature above, the time signature is 4/4 (four – four time) which is also known as common time. Instead of 4/4 you might see a "C" instead which indicates common time. The important thing to note here when you are starting out is that 4/4 time means that there will be 4 beats in each bar.

There are many types of times signatures in bagpipe music that you might come across. Some common examples are 2/4 (a.k.a. split common time, can be denoted as a "C" with a line through it), 3/4, 4/4, and 6/8

Details about different musical notes

When we are discussing different musical notes, the first thing to understand is how many beats each note is worth.

Each of the following notes indicates how many beats each note should be played for. For example, a semibreve (also known as a whole note) is made up of 4 beats, meaning that we will count 1-2-3-4 whilst playing this note. The minim (also known as a half-note) is 2 beats, a crotchet (also known as a quarter note) is one beat, and a quaver (also known as an eighth note) is half a beat.

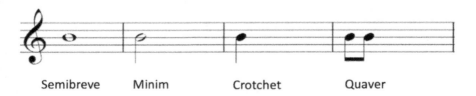

Semibreve   Minim   Crotchet   Quaver

Listening Example #1: Example of Different Musical Notes

The simplest way to start learning how to read rhythms is by thinking of each beat as a number. As we discussed in the previous section, the time signature will tell us how many beats there are in a bar (top number) and what note gets the beat (bottom number).

To start, a semibreve is made up for four beats. As such, we will count 1-2-3-4 while playing the note continuously. In this figure below, you can see that you can only have one semibreve in each bar as you can only have four beats in a bar.

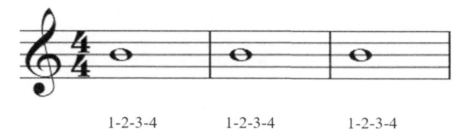

        1-2-3-4   1-2-3-4   1-2-3-4

In the next example, we have two minims in each bar. Each minim is two beats each and so we can have two minims in each bar and we will count 1-2 for the first minim and 3-4 for the second.

    1-2   3-4   1-2   3-4   1-2   3-4

In this example below, we have four crotchets in each bar. As one crotchet is worth one beat, we need to have 4 in the bar to

20

make it complete. As there are four beats in each bar, we count to four each time and then start over.

1   2   3   4   1   2   3   4   1   2   3   4

Once you start getting past the basics of bagpipe music, the next thing that you will see are notes that need to be played even faster. In the figure below, we still have 4 beats to a bar (denoted by the time signature 4/4) but this time the notes are quavers. Each quaver is only half a beat and therefore you need two quavers to make one beat. You can see that the way these are counted are 1 & 2 & 3 & 4 &.

1 & 2 & 3 & 4 &   1 & 2 & 3 & 4 &

Even though these are very basic notes, in music you will generally see many combinations of different note lengths to that make more interesting music. The thing to always remember is that your time signature will tell you how many beats there are in each bar and this is never going to change. The thing that will change is the different combination of notes that will make up each bar.

Learn about musical alphabets and basic notes

The musical alphabet is straightforward in that it follows the regular alphabet up until the letter G and then repeats. In the bagpipes, the notes are only in the key of D major, that is both C and F are played as sharp notes. However, as every piece of music is played in this key in bagpiping music, the key signature is usually not indicated on the sheet music. The other thing that makes it easier is that the scale (featured below) only has 9 notes from Low G to High A. You may think that only playing in one key signature and only 9 notes might make bagpiping music less interesting, however, the music has many more "embellishments" than other music.

Low G   A   B   C   D   E   F   G   High A

The simplest embellishment that you will come across is known as a "grace note." Other embellishments will be added into the music at the intermediate level.

Learn about musicianship skills

Musicianship skills are a set of skills that any musician has such as listening, humming music, playing, creating, reading, writing, ear training and much more. Similar to learning a language, learning how to play a new instrument is easier if you already know how to play an instrument already. If you already know how to read sheet music, you will likely find it easier to pick up a new instrument and learn how to play, than someone who doesn't know anything about music.

Developing musicianship skills is important for any new player. The ability to be able to hum a tune in your head, or figure out if a note sounds out of tune, are important skills but are also skills that can be learnt and refined with time. The more you play, are surrounded by music, and actively work on all aspects of musicianship skills, the quicker and better you will become at these skills.

Chapter 4

Playing Notes/Songs on the Practice Chanter

As you read in the previous section, it is best to start learning how to play the practice chanter before you begin playing the bagpipes. This will make your transition to the bagpipes much easier as you will be able to start with simple tunes when you transition over.

You can play only nine notes on a bagpipe.

One octave + 1 note -> nine notes (G, A, B, C, D, E, F, G, A) – low G to high G and high A

As we noted in the previous section, one of the great things about the bagpipes is that only nine notes can be played, beginning with the "low G" up to the "high A." This low G is the G above the middle C on the piano; as such, the octave we are playing in on the bagpipes fits nicely on the treble chef scale.

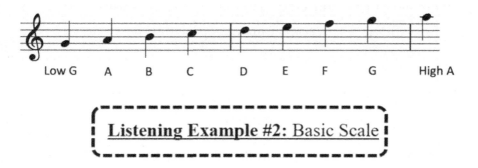

| Low G | A | B | C | D | E | F | G | High A |

No flats or sharps in Bagpipe music

When you come across bagpipe sheet music, you will probably notice that there are no flats or sharps listed. That is because bagpipe music is always played in the key of "D major." That's right; every tune is always played in D major, so flats and sharps are not usually listed on any sheet music. However, the D major key does have two sharps in it: F# and C#, so when you are playing bagpipe tunes, the notes F and C will always be sharp.

Practice playing notes (G, A, B, C, D, E, F, G, A) on the Chanter:

Practice finger positioning for each note

The first thing to note about finger positioning for each note is that it is not the tips of your fingers that are used to cover the holes on the chanter. In fact, you want to make sure that your fingers lay as flat as possible across the chanter. It might feel unnatural at first as different parts of your fingers will be covering the holes but it will become much easier with time.

Each note on the chanter is played differently and in a relatively logical sequence. From the figure below, you will see which holes you should cover to create each note.

Starting from the bottom of the scale, the simplest one to understand is the low G note where you will cover all of the holes with each of your fingers. Going up the scale, A, you release your right pinky finger, B, your right ring finger. Once you get to C, this is where it changes a little bit. You will release your middle finger but put down your pinky finger. It is important in bagpiping that you do put your pinky finger down to play C. In reality, the sound with or without the pinky down is very minor, but without it, you are doing something called "false fingering," and you won't maintain as much control. Moving to D you will release your right index finger.

After D, we move onto the left hand. The note E, you will release your left ring finger and put down your index, middle, and ring finger on your right hand at the same time, just leaving the pinky off. F, release the left middle finger, G, release the left index finger, and then for high A you will release your left thumb that has been covering the back hole, and put down your left ring finger.

It is important to note that for all of the changes going up and down the basic scale, that the movements happen at the same time. For example, when you move from D to E, you will put three fingers down on your right hand and take off one on the left. This movement needs to be completed all at the same time.

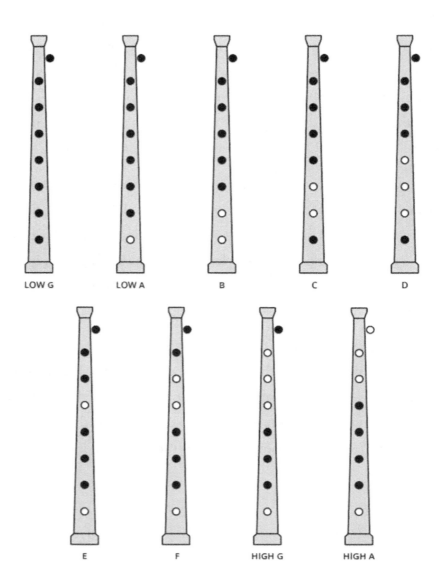

Finger positions on the chanter from Low G to High A

Exercises (with pictorial representations and music sheet)

Below are some basic exercises to get started. Each line builds in complexity so start with the top line and move on to the next line once you become comfortable with the previous. Starting with exercise A, this is just going up and down the scale starting on low G. One beat for each note.

Exercise B, this is the same as A but a little bit faster using quavers, going up and down the scale twice. You can repeat this as many times as you want until you become comfortable with going up and down the scale.

After you have completed exercises A and B, we are now going to learn the "grace note." Simply, the grace note is a quick lifting off of the finger and replacement. It is a very short and quick note and is a type of embellishment. Embellishments do not take away any beats from the main notes, they are there to add flavor to what you are playing. So, in exercise C, you will see that we are doing a G grace note (the grace note is on the G) so to do this you want to quickly tap your left index finger. Your finger should lift off the practice chanter and then back on quickly. When you are learning how to do this, just play the A note and practice lifting off and replacing your left index finger for the grace note. This type of grace note is the most common one that you will see.

The next exercise, you will see that we are practicing a D grace note. Same as before, but this time you will lift off your right index finger and replace it.

The third type of grace note to practice here is the E grace note. Same as the other two, you will lift off and replace your left ring finger.

Now, let's try and perform the first grace note going up and down the scale. This exercise is the same as the first scale, but this time each time you change notes you will also do a grace note.

Exercise G, you can practice the three types of grace notes that we have covered. Just stay playing the A note, and switch between the grace note styles.

The last exercise in this suite is a bit more complicated. The point of this exercise is to get you used to switching between notes that aren't right next to each other. So, going down the scale from high A and alternating with the A note. This exercise will also help you to think about which note you are going to play next.

Exercises 1

Composer

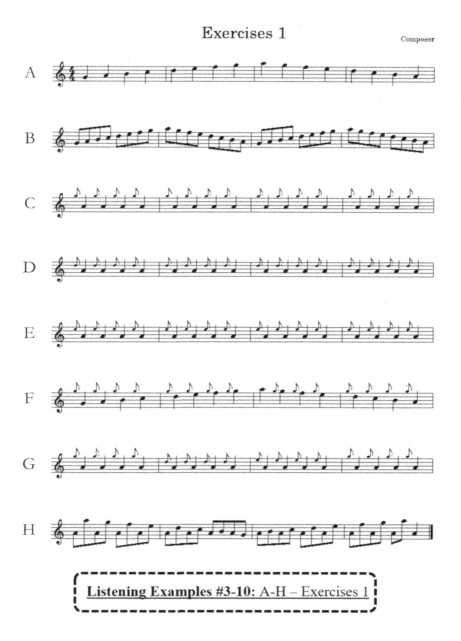

Practice playing simple songs by memorizing the notes

Exercises (with pictorial representations and music sheet)

Mary Had a Little Lamb

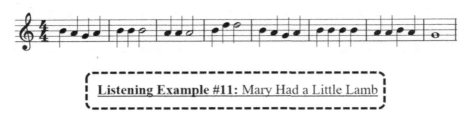

Listening Example #11: Mary Had a Little Lamb

Mary Had a Little Lamb (with grace notes)

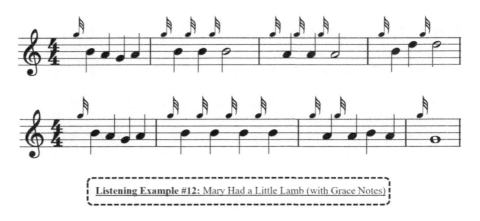

Listening Example #12: Mary Had a Little Lamb (with Grace Notes)

Frère Jacques

Listening Example #13: Frere Jacques

Use practice chanters to learn the notes

When you start playing the practice chanter it is important to learn the correct finger positioning for each note, however, maintaining good posture is also important. I would recommend first learning the correct position by looking and where your fingers are placed and then playing the notes and listening to how they sound. However, whilst you are playing the chanter don't look down at your fingers.

Instead of looking down at your fingers, you could use a mirror to watch.

The purpose of electronic chanters.

Depending on where you are and who is around you, a normal chanter can be loud to listen to. Some players have opted to buy an electric chanter to practice on. You can plug headphones into it and you don't have to blow into it. It is easy to transport and nobody can hear you practice. While electric chanters are good, they generally don't feel like a practice chanter or a bagpipe chanter. The holes are generally electrodes that are used to know where the players fingers are so the indentation of an actual chanter usually isn't there.

It is recommended to use an actual practice chanter when you are learning to play the bagpipes. Not only will it help to mimic more what the pipe chanter will feel like but you will also build up a bit of stamina while having to blow into the practice chanter. This will help when you move onto the bagpipes.

Chapter 5

Bagpipe Basics - Parts of a Bagpipe (with pictorial representations)

Now that you have successfully understood the basics of playing the practice chanter, it is time to move on to the main event. Let's start by looking at a set of bagpipes, breaking down the individual parts, and discussing how they are used.

When you first pick up a set of bagpipes, you may be terrified of all the moving parts and pieces that go into them. Fear not! Although they look complicated at the beginning, once you begin to understand the function of each part and how to hold your bagpipes, they will become much simpler.

Bag

The bag is the main part of the bagpipes. The bag is essentially a holding cell for the air that will be pushed through the reeds to create sounds from the pipes. As the bagpipes are composed of three drones and a chanter, you will need to play all these four things simultaneously. The bag is connected to the drones and chanter. By blowing into the bag and filling the bag up, you can simultaneously push air through these different parts to create various sounds.

Furthermore, when you are playing the bagpipes, there will be a constant sound coming from the drones and the chanter. However, while blowing into the bagpipes, you will need to breathe at some point! Squeezing the bag while you are taking a breath allows for the continuation of the drones and chanter and, thus, will enable you to play your song (more on this later) continuously.

Two main types of bags are commonly used: skin and synthetic. When I say skin, I also mean leather. Traditionally, the bag of the bagpipes is made of sheepskin. However, there are also bags out there that are made of goat, cow, elk, or even dog skin. In recent decades, synthetic bags have become increasingly common and popular, but how they feel when you play varies from that of a leather bag.

Blowstick/blowpipe

The blowstick/blowpipe is the part of the bagpipes you blow in to fill the bag. This is an integral part of the bagpipes, and the length of the blowpipe should be chosen for the individual player. If you are a little shorter (or if it's for a child) and the distance between your mouth and the bag is small, you will want a slightly shorter blowpipe. And if you are taller, a longer blowpipe may suit you better.

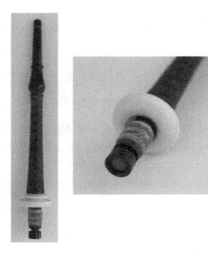

Blowpipe/stick. Can be easily removed from the bagpipes
and will contain a valve at the base for one way airflow.

The fit of the blowpipe into the bagpipes themselves is also important (refer to chapter 8 for more information on connections and how to adjust the fit). The blowpipe needs to fit snugly to prevent any leaks from happening.

The other part of the blowpipe worth mentioning is the valve at the end that sits just inside the bag. This valve is usually delicate and should not be removed. If it is broken off, you will need to replace it. This valve ensures that no air can escape from the bag when you are taking a breath but is delicate enough that you can easily blow into the bag.

Drones

Three drones rest on the player's left shoulder and are used to create an accompanying sound (pitch and tone) in the background of the melody, two tenor drones, and one bass drone. These three drones are tuned to play the note "A." This note will work for all music while playing the bagpipes, as the melody played on the chanter will almost always be in the key of D major.

Drones are powered by drone reeds which are within each of the drones at the base. Each drone can be removed from the bag at the base, and the reed is attached to the bottom of the drone.

For tuning purposes, the outside tenor drone is usually the first drone to be tuned, followed by the bass, and finally the middle tenor.

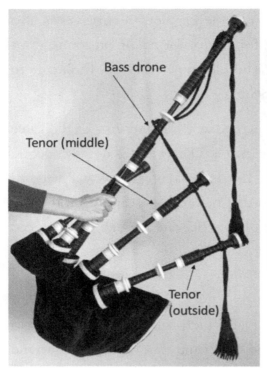

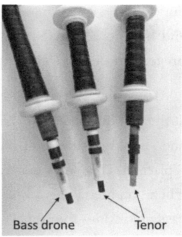

Bagpipes and tenor reeds

One Bass Drone - Plays low A

The bass drone is the largest of the three drones and sits on top of the shoulder, close to the player's ear. This drone has three components and two moving parts, one at the top of the drone and the other by the player's ear. The main moving part to focus on is this one in the middle next to the player's ear. This part of the drone is used for tuning and can be twisted up and down to tune the individual drone.

Two Tenor Drones - Plays middle A

The tenor drones are the same and will play a middle "A" note. They only have one moving part that is used for tuning the drone. When you start learning how to play a full set of the bagpipes, it is typical for the middle tenor drone to be blocked off until the player builds up enough stamina to be able to play all three drones simultaneously. You can either block off the middle tenor by replacing the reed with a rubber cork on the inside, or when you start the bagpipes up, you can force it to shut by holding your finger over the hole at the top for a few seconds and it will stop. This second method is a less permanent fix, so I would recommend that when you are starting, block the middle tenor off with a rubber cork.

Drone Cords

You may think that the drone cords are purely just for looks, but they, in fact, play a very important role. The drone cords are used to hold all three of the drones together so that the bagpipes can easily be played without the drones moving too much.

Drone cords come in various colors, but generally, all look very similar. It is common that bands will all have the same drone cords for consistency and may choose to tie the long cord that hangs off the bass drone into an elegant knot.

Cable ties are usually used between drones to hold each drone in place. These cable ties can be cut and re-positioned if you need to move the drones closer together or further apart. The goal is for the drones to sit comfortably across the player's shoulder and top of their left arm without hanging too far down.

Chanter

The chanter is what is used to play the melody. As discussed in chapter 1 and 2, the practice chanter is what you will start learning before you move on to playing the full set of bagpipes. There are a couple of main differences between your practice chanter (depending on which style you have) and a chanter on the bagpipes.

Firstly, your practice chanter may or may not have an additional hole at the bottom that runs perpendicular to the other holes. This feature will definitely be present on your bagpipe chanter.

Secondly, the holes on the bagpipe chanter will likely be bigger than those on your practice chanter. Each note on your bagpipe chanter can be slightly tuned individually using a piece of tape, usually at the top of the hole. Pipe majors may choose to tune each player's chanter to provide more consistency within the band. As a learner, this is not something you need to worry about, but down the line, you may want to learn how to tune your chanter.

And lastly, the reed that is used within the chanter will likely be different. Usually, a wooden reed is used in a bagpipe chanter and a smaller plastic reed in a practice chanter.

Four Reeds – A device that produces a tone due to vibration (caused by airflow)

There are four reeds that are used to power the sound of the bagpipes. Three are used for the drones and the last for the chanter.

The style of drone reeds varies slightly between styles and brands; however, pipers usually play synthetic drone reeds as they are more easily adjusted. The bass drone reed is larger than the two tenor reeds (identical), and depending on the style, the bass reed may look different. Drone reeds are built with a tongue that is usually larger and maybe a bit thicker on the bass drone.

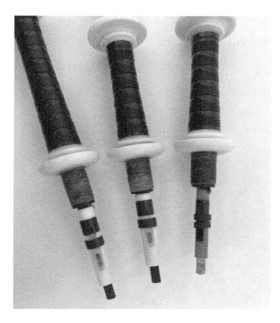

Drone reeds. Base reed on the left and two tenor reeds in the middle and right

Depending on the piper, the tongue of the drone reed can be adjusted to create the perfect sound for each piper. This is important because some pipers can push more air through their drones than others. This can cause the drones to shut off or squeal; however, this can be avoided by adjusting the drone.

Bagpipes' chanter reed is made of wood and looks more similar to the reeds you may be used to seeing on other instruments. Two pieces of thin wood are wrapped tightly together at the base, and sound is created when air is pushed through the top. Similar to the drone reeds, some players will be able to push more air through the chanter reed, and as such, they will need a thicker reed to create the best sound. If the piper isn't able to push as much air through the reed, the edges of the reed can be slightly shaved down (with a small knife or razor) to create a thinner reed that is easier to play. I would recommend getting help with this if you haven't done it before, as the tip of the reed is very delicate and easily damaged. You don't want to shave down too much, either.

Pipe chanter reed — wooden

Chapter 6

Learning the Bagpipe Basics

Once you have started to play a few simple tunes on the practice chanter and can confidently hold the practice chanter and blow through a tune or two, you will be ready to take the next step and move on to the bagpipes. It is essential that you can hold the practice chanter correctly and can play a few tunes before starting with the bagpipes. This is because adding the drones and the bag adds additional layers of complexity and can be confusing, to begin with.

We will start with learning how to set up your bagpipes and then move through the various steps until we can play a simple tune.

How to set up your bagpipes

The setup process may vary slightly depending on whether you have bought a second-hand or completely new set of bagpipes. Generally, if you have purchased a new set of pipes, all the individual pieces may be separated and require you to put them together. If you have bought a set of second-hand bagpipes, they will likely be already set up, so we will first discuss how bagpipes are stored between practice sessions.

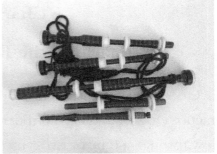

Bagpipes can be disassembled either partially or fully. You may find they need to be completely or partially disassembled for transport and storage in their case.

In its most basic case, usually, the top half of the bass drone will be detached (where the bass drone is tuned), the chanter will be removed, and a protective case will be placed over the top of the chanter reed. As such, when you open the case and remove the bagpipes, you will need to put the bass drone back together, remove the protective case from the chanter, and carefully place the chanter into the bagpipes. Don't worry about the tuning of the bass drone at this point; just place it on roughly in this position, and we will tune it later. With the chanter, when you carefully place it into the bagpipes, you will want to ensure that the finger holes are facing forwards. The position of the finger holes can be changed later on, but you can roughly guess their position when you first start. Some players may also choose to remove the blowpipe each time, so you may need to attach this as well. Tip: once you have started playing your bagpipes, you will figure out a comfortable position for your chanter, and you can place a piece of tape over the top of the chanter and bottom of the connection so that every time you set up your bagpipes, you can easily find the perfect position for your chanter.

If you have bought a new set of bagpipes or have a much smaller carry case, you may find that most of the bagpipes have been disassembled and require more assembling before you play. The tops of the drones will be connected by the drone cords, which will be attached to the main part of the drone via the tuning connection. The drones will be connected to the bag with the drone reeds sitting inside.

Learning how to start the bagpipes and hold them correctly

When you are learning how to hold the bagpipes, there are two main positions and one transition move that you need to understand. As you get used to feeling the bagpipes, you can use both hands to adjust the position. It is important to understand that to start the bagpipes, and you will need to learn to essentially jump-start the engine, so to speak. Unlike other instruments, the bagpipes require a quick rush of air through the drones to get them started. As such, the first position requires the player to be in this position for the attack. Once the bagpipes are started, you will have to move the position to play.

The first position that we will discuss is the starting position before you inflate the bagpipes and start playing. The second position is where you will move the bagpipes to begin playing.

Start by placing the bagpipes over your left shoulder with the base drone resting on the top of your shoulder. The bag should be low between your body and arm at this stage (you don't want the bag right up under your armpit). You want to place the blowstick in your mouth and hold the top of the chanter with your left hand. Specifically, you want to place your first three fingers on the top three holes and the back hole using your left hand. Your right hand should be placed inside the bag, ready for attack.

To inflate the bag, you simply need to blow into the blowstick. The end of the blowstick has a small rubber valve that prevents air from leaving the bag as you blow into it. Air can still escape through the reeds, but you will notice that the bag will inflate pretty easily when you first start blowing into it.

To make the attack, you want to squeeze the bag with your left arm and right hand in a relatively aggressive way. Think of it as a jump-start. It needs to be firm and quick. As soon as you have initiated this attack, you want to keep blowing into the bag. The next step is moving the bag into the second position, as mentioned in the previous section while blowing and squeezing the bag to keep the bagpipes going.

The next position is the one you will take once you have "jump-started" the bagpipes (which we will discuss next). After jump-starting the drones, you will use your right hand to push the bag up underneath your armpit. You want the bag to be far up enough that you can easily squeeze it with your left arm, but placing it too far up will feel uncomfortable. After practicing this a couple of times, you will figure out how far up you need to push the bag to make for a comfortable position.

Preparation   Atack   Playing

Approximate positions for starting the bagpipes beginning with preparation followed by attack, and into playing position.

Learning to control your breath while blowing into the blowpipe

The bagpipes are controlled by a combination of blowing into the bag as well as squeezing the bag. The goal here is to maintain constant pressure through the drones and chanter. Bagpipe music rarely has any rests or time where you are not playing. As such, it is crucial that we are constantly playing. To do this, you will blow into the bag, and while taking a breath, you will squeeze the bag, blow back into the bag to inflate it, squeeze again, and so on.

The start practicing this, you can start the bagpipes and simply practice blowing and squeezing without making a noise with the chanter. You will be able to hear the sound of the drones and learn how to try and make this motion as consistent as possible. When you are blowing into the bagpipes, you should try and blow firmly and consistently.

Understand that air, pressure, and deflation are directly related to the type of bag (skin or synthetic)

As mentioned previously, skin (hide or hybrid) bags are more common amongst pipers. They bring more of a traditional feel than synthetic bags and the way they are played is slightly different. Once you have tried both a synthetic and skin bag, you will understand the feel difference between the two. Generally speaking, the skin bags are thicker and feel more "sturdy" in terms of playing. The synthetic bags tend to require a bit more arm movement as they expand and contract as you are playing.

Practice controlling your breath and left arm

When you are blowing into the bag, you want to try and create a balance between blowing into the bag and whilst you are taking a breath, squeezing the bag with your left arm. The goal here is to create a consistent flow of air through the drones. A steady sound is what makes for great bagpipers.

Something to look out for is that you don't want to puff your cheeks up. Developing an embouchure in bagpipes doesn't really exist. You just want the mouth piece in your mouth and to blow strongly into the bag. Puffing your cheeks out won't help with blowing into the bag, it will likely make it more difficult.

Learn how to properly close the eight holes in the chanter with your left and right fingers

As you will know how to play basic notes and tunes on the practice chanter, the next step is to do this on the bagpipes. The holes on the bagpipe chanter will be slightly larger than what you are likely used to seeing on the practice chanter. Start by starting up the bagpipes and playing a low "A" note. Ensure all your fingers cover the holes except your right pinky finger. Then try playing a low "G" note so that your fingers cover all the holes. From here, you can try playing a scale starting with low G all the way up to high A and back down again.

Briefly understand the mechanics of how a bagpipe makes a sound.

The bagpipes make sound through the drones and the chanter. Much like other woodwind instruments, they produce sound by pushing air through reeds which causes the reed to vibrate and the air in the "resonator" produces sound. In the case of the bagpipes, the drones and the chanter are the resonators.

The big difference with the bagpipes and other woodwind instruments is the reservoir (bag) that is used to store air. This allows for air to be constantly pushed through the drones and chanter allowing for a constant sound.

Briefly understand how to tune your drones

When you are starting out learning how to play the drones, it really is best to get someone from a pipeband to tune your drones for you. It can be a little bit complicated to tune on your own. However, if you are learning by yourself and need to tune your drones this is what you should do.

You first want to start up your bagpipes. Start my blocking off your bass and middle tenor drone as we will first tune the outside tenor drone. To do this you should listen to the drone. It is probably making an inconsistent sound, fluctuating between two noises. The ideas here is to make this inconsistency go away and the drone to make one consistent noise. A tuner can be used to do this but when you are on your own you only have two hands to do this. So, playing the chanter you want to play a high-A note and use your right hand to tune the drone. Essentially just keep moving the tuning joint up or down until the drone makes one consistent noise. That's when you know you are in tune (or as close to in tune as we are going to get). You can then do the same thing with the bass drone. Block off the outside tenor that we just tuned and then tune the bass. Repeat the same process for the tenor.

This method will allow you to get your drones as close to in tune as you can on your own. But also note that the weather conditions can make your drones go out of tune so it is important to continue to check the tuning.

Chapter 7

Introduction to Intermediate Techniques

Taking the next step in your bagpipe playing is to learn how to read and understand other embellishments that you may come across. This is especially important if you are looking to play more complicated tunes and play in a pipeband.

Learn the striking technique (seems advanced but something useful while playing in a band)

The striking technique, also known as the D strike, is a type of embellishment that you will often see. In fact, it is one of the first embellishments played in "Amazing Grace." The D strike is a relatively simple technique that is easier to play than the embellishment looks on sheet music (see below).

D strike

> **Listening Example #14:** DStrike – Intermediate Techniques

To play the D-strike, all you really need to do is play a D note and then quickly tap your right index, middle, and ring finger on the chanter. What you are doing is essentially making a grace note on the note D.

Learning how to play "D throw"

From intermediate music and above, you will see "D throws" everywhere. They are a very common embellishment that every intermediate player should know how to play, especially for music often played in a pipeband.

Like other embellishments, the easiest way to start is to break it down into the components. The sequence for playing a D throw is easiest if you start on the low A note. From low A, we go to low G, D, C, D. Every time you play a D throw you will be placing all of your fingers down in the low G position before the D, C, D component. Start by practicing from low A and take it slowly. As you get used to the order of the notes, you can increase your speed and get it fast enough. I would recommend listening to how a D throw is supposed to sound as it will help you get a feeling of what you are aiming for.

D throw

Listening Example #15: DThrow – Intermediate Techniques

After you have mastered playing a D throw starting from the low A note, you can try and play a D throw from all of the other notes, going up and down the scale.

Quick introduction to other embellishments

Embellishments are generally made up of grace notes on G, D, and E as well closing all of the holes on the low G note.

There are a few other embellishments that you may come across. One in particular to note is a "birl." If you play a low A note, a birl is a quick low G, low A note embellishment (see below). Unlikely some of the other embellishments that we have talked about, there are two main techniques that players use for the birl. Either you can use your pinky to tap the low G note and then pull off, or you can use your pinky to slide up and down over the low G note. Which technique you use is players choice and both are equally used by many players.

Birl

Listening Example #16: Birl – Intermediate Techniques

Now that we have walked through a variety of embellishments, you should understand how to read different embellishments in sheet music and will be able to pick up on any new embellishments that you may come across. Below is an example of an embellishment that we haven't talked about yet. From the notes alone, can you figure out how to play it?

Embellishments

Listening Example #17: Embellishment – Intermediate Techniques

The key to playing this particular embellishment is that you are starting on an E note, you will then play a low G, grace note on D and then back to E. This type of embellishment is usually called "doubling" and you can do something like this with a variety of notes and grace note combinations. The key here is that you can understand how to read the notes and from there you will be able to play many other embellishments that you may come across!

Chapter 8

Caring For Your Bagpipes

The Bag

There are some essential things to know about looking after your bag. When you first buy a new bag, it will need to be seasoned. This is particularly important for leather bags. Like leather shoes and bags, you will need to keep up on maintenance to keep them in good condition and sealed from air and harsh weather conditions. As such, after the initial seasoning, you will then season (also called dressing) the bag again after about a week.

How often you dress your bag after this depends on your environment and how much you play your bagpipes. As a general rule of thumb, about every 4-6 weeks should do the trick. You should be able to find a seasoning/dressing to buy from several bagpipe manufacturers and sellers.

All you need to do to season your bag is remove the drones, blow stick/pipe, and chanter and plug all the holes with rubber corks. Then pour some of the seasoning solution into the bag, either through one of the holes or if the bag has a zip on the side, you can pour it in there. Next, give it a good slosh around and rub the sides of the bag against each other to really rub the solution into the bag. You can then drain out any excess and put back all the drones and chanter.

Water trap & moisture control

Maintaining control over your moisture in a bagpipe set-up is important in order to keep the reeds from becoming saturated. The simplest system is to add a water trap into your set-up. A water trap is a tube that attaches on the inside of the bag to the blowstick. It essentially catches moisture in the tube and you can drain it out after playing.

Airtight – hemp wax thread

The last and important piece of information that you should know in caring for your bagpipes is making your bagpipes airtight. Every connection in your bagpipes should have hemp wax thread that is used to make a tight connection. Hemp wax is usually used as it makes it easier to twist the connections on and off (especially for tuning the drones and storage) and it is also more resistant to moisture. The stick of the hemp also really helps with the seal.

To add hemp thread to the blowpipe, you want to take the thread and wrap it around the blowpipe all over the connection. Keep layering on the thread until you reach a snug fit of the blowpipe into the bag.

General maintenance

In between playing your bagpipes, it is totally ok to break them down and store them in a case. Most cases will only require that you remove the chanter and the top half of the bass drone to store it in the case. Ideally if you are in more humid conditions, it is better to not store your bagpipes in these humid conditions as it is not great for the wood. You can add a canister of kitty litter into your pipe case if this is a real problem but generally speaking just storing them in the case out of the heat is good enough.

Chapter 9

Preparing to Play in a Pipeband

Different types of songs in Bagpipe music

Let's briefly discuss different types of songs in bagpipe music and how they fit together. This information if more for intermediate level or if you are looking to join a pipeband.

In bagpipe repertoire, there are different categories that we can break down different tunes into. Independent pieces of music are called "tunes." You can also play tunes of similar type in what is called a "set" or a "medley." To make this similar, we can talk about bagpipe competition. In competition, pipebands are required to play a set, medley, and street march for judges who will determine which band played each of these the best. A set usually consists of a March + Strathspey + Reel (MSR).

MSR (March + Strathspey + Reel)

March: Typically played in 4/4 (common time), 2/4 time, or less commonly 2/2 time. A march, like the name suggests, is a piece of music that is commonly played in the style of a marching band. The rhythm is generally relatively simple and can easily be marched to.

Strathspey: A strathspey is a higher tempo piece of music that is commonly known as a "dance tune." Although strathspeys are typically and upbeat piece of music, they are generally slower than a reel. Here, it is noted that strathspeys create a "rhythmic tension" that is released by playing a reel the strathspey.

Reel: Finally, a reel is played at the end of an MSR and is usually the fastest tempo played in this set. Reels are played with even beats usually in 4/4 or 2/2 time with the emphasis on the first and third notes in the bar.

Medley (could be any combination such as march, strathspey, reel, slow-air, hornpipes and jigs are common but no set structure).

A medley generally is less structured and bands typically can have more fun with it and play more fun tunes. An example of a medley could be that the band is going to play a march, reel, slow-air, hornpipe, and jig.

Slow-air: A slow-air like the name suggests is usually a relatively short piece of music that is played relatively slowly. Although a variety of tempos could work here, slow-airs usually are played in 6/8 or 3/4 time. If a band is going to add in harmony, a slow-air is the perfect place to do it. It is common to see bands build up to a slow-air in the middle of a medley and then dive into the fun hornpipes and jigs in the back-half of their medley. It is almost kind of used as a time to breathe and slow-down before launching into the faster, fun tunes.

Hornpipe: Hornpipes are another fun style of music that have a dance feel to them. Although they are similar in tempo to a reel, hornpipes usually have an implied dotted rhythm to them, meaning they are played with a "swung" feeling. Usually written in 4/4 time.

Jig: Jigs are fun pieces of music to play and dance along to. Pipebands usually use these towards the end of a medley before abruptly finishing at the end. If you watch any of the competitive pipebands, you will see they often end with a fun piece of music like a jig and the abrupt ending makes for an excellent show. Many jigs are played in 6/8 timing and are usually fast and upbeat.

Street March

A street march is usually something that the band can play easily whilst walking down the street in formation, such as what you would see at a parade. It is very common for a band to play a street march which is in 3/4 or 4/4 time signatures.

Music sheet for Popular melodies and songs (all-time favorites)

If you end up joining a pipeband, they will give you a repertoire that will include many all-time favorites that all pipers typically know. However, here is a few to get you started. Amazing Grace is a tune that every piper should know. It is great for a variety of occasions and is one of those classic songs that you will often hear.

Another classic that is played often is Scotland the Brave. It is one of those tunes that everybody knows and can play with other bands on command without warning. If someone asks you to play a fun, classic bagpipe song, Scotland the Brave is probably the one I would go for.

Lastly, A Hundred Pipers. As the title suggests, this is a great tune for something called "massed bands." At pipeband competitions, generally, at the end of the last day all of the bands will come together and play a tune together. This can be literally more than a hundred pipers and drummers. It is such a fun tune to play, and playing with hundreds of other pipers in a massed band it such a fun experience. So, this tune is definitely on the list as one that you should know when you join a pipeband.

Scotland The Brave

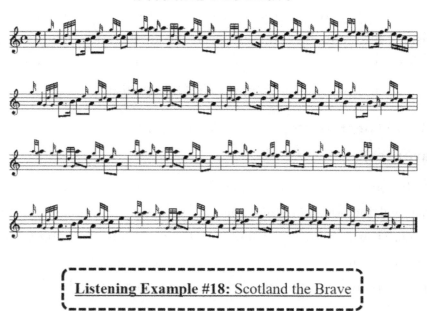

Listening Example #18: Scotland the Brave

Although bagpipe music varies between styles, the overall structure remains relatively the same. It is common that you will see music written in "measures," usually 4 bars in the first line and 4 in the second. As in other music, the measures and bars within the measures denote a question in the first line and a resolution in the second. Many tunes are comprised of multiple parts. In the example of "A Hundred Pipers" below you will see that the first two lines are repeated, followed by the second two lines. It should be noted that the first and second bars of line 1 and 2 are the same but bars 3 and 4 are different. This structure is relatively common and the idea of questions and answers is used very frequently and in a structured way.

A Hundred Pipers

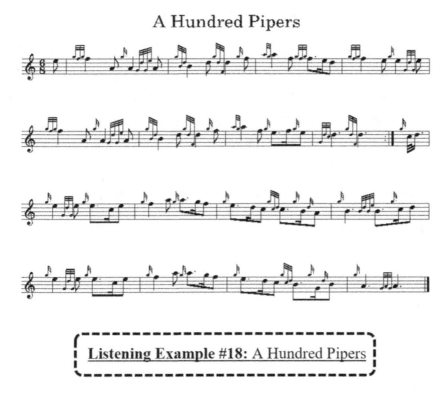

Listening Example #18: A Hundred Pipers

If you are looking for more sheet music to learn, some other popular tunes that you may here around include: Flower of Scotland, Highland Cathedral, and Highland Wedding. Some of these tunes may be a little difficult to play at first. As such, I would recommend starting slow and playing along with a recording online to help get a feel for the tune.

The great thing about bagpipe music is that the tunes are pretty much universal. Some bands may play very slight variations on these tunes but overall, the sheet music isn't going to change all that much. So, it is very easy to look online for sheet music for any song that you might want to learn how to play.

Exercises to Build Techniques and to play in a band

When you are looking to build your techniques to be able to play in a pipeband, the most important thing that you can learn is how to play in time and on beat. Pipebands are a little bit about the cool tunes that the band plays but it is so much more about playing the same tunes at the same time as all other pipers. It is about playing on time, with the drum core, and everything happening in unison. To do this, you should practice all of your exercises with a metronome.

Below are some more exercises to continue building technique.

Exercises 2

Composer

A

B

C

D

E

F

G

Listening Examples #20-26: A-H – Exercises 2

Chapter 10

Conclusion

Learning how to play the bagpipes can be a great way to challenge yourself and learn an instrument that has a deep Scottish rooted history. It can be an incredibly rewarding experience and will allow you to meet many people in the pipeband world.

I would recommend that anyone out there looking to learn how to play the bagpipes joins a pipeband as soon as possible. Not only is it a great way to learn how to play the bagpipes (surrounded by other learners with teachers) but it is a fun and rewarding experience and it may take you to locations that you never thought about. Pipebands often compete at local competitions, you will get to wear a uniform, and meet plenty of other pipers in the process.

Appendix

Additional Resources

Troubleshooting tips & advice

Struggling to maintain a full bag of air

One of the most common problems that you may come across is not being able to maintain a pull bag of air. If this happens, the first thing to check is that all of our connections are tight enough. Tight enough so that you can still twist them but not so loose that air could be escaping through the gaps. The other thing to check is that the reeds are still in place. If the reeds are not secure, they can loosen and even fall out. Using beeswax hemp can help fix both of these problems.

F and C notes are always sharp, except...

I mentioned that in bagpipe music, F and C are always sharp as we always play in D major. This is true. However, you may come across one or two music pieces with a natural F or natural C. It is very uncommon to see this, but it does exist. Fingering for F natural and C natural here.

More exercises and sheet music

If you are looking for more sheet music and songs to play here is a list of online resources where you could look:

Google is a great place to start. You can find many pieces of music online for free to play.

https://pipetunes.ca
https://bagpipemusic.com

Unlock Your Musical Potential: Get 30% Off the Next Step in Your Instrumental Journey

As a token of appreciation for your dedication, we're excited to offer you an **exclusive 30% discount** on your next product when you sign up below with your email address.

Click the link below:
https://bit.ly/40NikR2
OR
Use the QR Code:

Unlocking your musical potential is easier with ongoing guidance and support. Join our community of passionate musicians to elevate your skills and stay updated with the latest tips and tricks.

By signing up, you'll also receive our periodic newsletter with additional insights and resources to enhance your musical journey.

Your privacy is important to us. We won't spam you, and you can unsubscribe anytime.

Don't miss out on this opportunity to continue your musical journey with this special discount. Sign up now, and let's embark on this musical adventure together! 𝄞

Made in United States
Orlando, FL
01 July 2025

62531692R10046